I LO.. WHEN...

BY RICHARD COMBES

ILLUSTRATED BY PETER STANDLEY

Nightingale Press

an imprint of Wimbledon Publishing Company Ltd.

LONDON

First published in Great Britain
by Wimbledon Publishing Co. Ltd
London P.O. Box 9779 SW19 7ZG

ISBN: 1903222 36 2

Produced in Great Britain
Printed and bound in Hungary

...when she weeps rivers for the sickly domestic pets featured on Animal Hospital; and then coos with amazement and delight as they all make full recoveries. Like anything else was going to happen.

...when she gives the same level of care to me as she does to the kids. Although dinner with the boss was probably not the best time to spit on a hankie and scrub the food from the side of my mouth.

...when she teaches me the art of diplomacy. Do say: 'That's a lovely new hairdo, darling, it's so this season.' Don't say: 'And judging by the hurricane windblown effect, I'm guessing the season in question must be Autumn.'

...when she transforms the bathroom into a pharmacy cum health and beauty salon. If ever a herd of dyspeptic rhino should happen by in need of a damn good exfoliate and moisturise - we'll be ready for them.

...when she keeps my feet on the ground. I'm standing there brandishing a masonry hammer, looking dangerously virile in my dangling tool-belt, fondling the walls, looking for the best point at which to 'knock through'. Then I hear the voice of reason call, 'Honey, have you hung that picture up yet?'

...when she makes a visit to a restaurant more instructive than a day at school. Having painstakingly translated every item on the menu from the French, she then provides a breakdown as to their constituent saturated fat levels, before finishing by describing the cardiovascular damage each will inflict. Yum.

...when she sees the bright side of everything. 'My car's been sounding a bit cranky for the last few days - but a sweet little picture of a watering can has started flashing.'

...when she applies unanswerable logic to life's great mysteries. 'If all the little men kicked the same way, wouldn't they score more goals? Why don't they just use more balls?'

...when she believes that honesty is the best policy. Like in the fast-food restaurant - handing over a week's pay for a paper sack containing two French fries, a sip of coke, a chicken nugget and a vast, gaudily-coloured chunk of Taiwanese plastic: 'Exactly what is it about this meal that's "happy" then?'

..,when she's mindful of my well-being. I'm certain to come to no harm on the roads with her in the passenger seat; pointing out cyclists up to a radius of two hundred feet, pedestrians several miles away and sometimes even hazardous-looking trees.

...when she helps me to enjoy the good things in life. In moderation. So when we're out I get regular bulletins updating me on the number of units of alcohol I have consumed and the potential damage to my health and safety. It's like being out with a WPC and nurse at the same time. Now there's a thought.

...when she speaks my language. I say, 'What's wrong, darling?' She says, 'I need a whole new wardrobe.' I say, 'Okay, pine or rosewood?' She says, 'Ho, ho.' And hits me with a blunt instrument.

...when she corrects my misconceptions. For example, a combination diet apparently doesn't mean simply combining everything in the fridge into a mixing bowl, dousing it with brown sauce and then piping it between two thick, white crusts.

...when she says those special things.
Like when we lie entwined together, basking
in the warmth of that special 'after moment',
she turns to me, and with a look of wonder in
her eyes whispers those three little words:
'Is that it?'

...when she loses all sense of judgement and ability for rational thought at the mention of the three magic words: *Revolutionary New Diet.* 'With this one you can eat all the peas you want, and anything else so long as it's on toast and you combine eggs with nuts. Or is that nuts with eggs?'

...when she helps me with vital areas of the kids' education. 'When will Daddy be finished testing our new Playstation, Mummy?' 'Either at the end of this level or when he's finished drooling over Lara Croft, dear. Why don't you read a nice book while you're waiting?'

...when she enlivens my senses. No trip to the Body Shop would be complete without her passing three hundred soap samplers beneath my nostrils accompanied by the earnest enquiry, 'Mmm?'

...when she nurses me through illness. Anyone who can put up with Olympic-standard whining, Oscar-winning self-pity and mountains of mucus-encrusted tissues is surely one in a million.

...when she understands the male psyche. So even though she knows that I love her more than anything in the world, I am only obliged to admit as much after several vats of export-strength lager. It's the law.

...when she leaves sweet, little notes for me around the house. Like the one I found the other day attached to the toilet seat, 'Leave this up again and I'm moving to Latvia with the kids.'

...when she illustrates the theory of relativity in a simple, everyday context. Like how the phrase, 'I just need a couple of minutes to get ready' actually means, 'Sit down, pour yourself a drink and get incredibly comfortable.'

...when she cooks my favourite meal. Maybe one day she'll understand my fondness for Arabic culture and realise that the hefty belch that always follows is a mark of respect, appreciation and gratitude. And love.

...when she explains the realities of life. Like, that although diamonds are a girl's best friend, she is more than prepared to hang out with family bars of Fruit 'n' Nut and large glasses of chilled white wine should they ever visit.

...when she understands the basic hunter/gatherer instinct in me. So now, 'Don't worry about supper tonight dear, just leave it to me.' receives the response, 'Oh, okay, well make mine a 12 inch Hawaiian with garlic bread, and don't forget to tip the delivery boy.'

...when she explains the mysteries of the universe to me. So when I'm gazing dumbfounded into the washing machine drum, she talks me through the rule of physics whereby socks entering the wash cycle as a pair, always fuse into one.
Sod's first law of sockage.

...when she has her little joke. Like when I ask if she's finished changing the baby and she explains that, 'no, I still have plenty of room for improvement.'

...when she sets me little challenges. What could be easier than shopping for her favourite shampoo? 'I think this is the right one, it has a pre-wash semi-conditioning formula that individually de-gibblifies each follicle. Sorry I took so long - I had to sit a doctorate in microbiology before I could read the label.'

...when she surprises me with those little, but oh-so-important things. Like snuggling over to my side of the bed, on a Saturday morning lie-in and whispering softly into my ear, a 'little' list of oh-so-important things that need doing around the house.

...when she's ingenious. It was her that invented *The Car Journey Junior Olympics*, featuring: the 15,000m Silence, the Stay Putt, and the Slumber Marathon.

...when she appreciates my efforts. 'Mmm, darling this tastes really good. It's surprising how well cottage cheese and pilchards go together. I suppose the ketchup helps; maybe next time a little less curry powder...'

...when she can communicate without the need for words. A long, lingering, soulful glance tells me, 'I think you're the most wonderfully kind, special, caring, beautiful man alive.' Either that or 'Have you taken that bloody rubbish out yet?'
Those two are very similar.

...when she delights in my little jokes. She says, 'I just haven't got any shoes.' I dash upstairs, look in the cupboard and reply, 'Don't worry darling, some kindly travelling shoe elves have left you 200 used pairs.' Shortly after, one of the pairs is travelling towards my head at high speed.

...when she guides me through the maze of life. Sitting there in the passenger seat, brow furrowed, eyes darting wildly between the roadmap and the windscreen, she says 'I'm guessing from the herd of sheep in the distance that this isn't the M1.'

...when she improves my social skills.
I now realise that an accidental breakage of
wind in mixed company is not remedied by the
phrase, 'Steady on Vicar.'

...when she values my opinion.
Like when we're out clothes shopping. As
long as I remember that, 'Do you like this?'
ranks alongside some of the greatest
philosophical quandaries known to man.
There really is no right answer.

...when she's diplomatic. 'It's not that I dislike spending time with your family. It's more of a fiercely intense loathing.'

...when she introduces me to new people -
'Darling, this is Miss Mop, her life partner,
Mr Bucket and their little boy Brillo.
Oh look, here comes Mr Sheen - I don't
believe you've met.'

`

...when she reads my thoughts and I can read hers. So when we're in a bookshop, I head off to browse through the work of S.A.S.-trained former mercenaries, she seeks out a tale of a thirty-something city girl fixated by her: weight, self, intake of booze/choc/fags, who - via a series of perky high jinks - finally gets her man.

...when she puts together all the elements of a perfect romantic dinner. Fine wines, sumptuous food, soft lighting, a little light background music and, the *pièce de résistance*, Ceefax in the corner scrolling down the football scores.

...when she broadens my vocabulary. Most notably after a gruelling marathon of TV cookery. 'Okay darling, tonight we're having warmed pancetta, drizzled in rustic guacamole, streaked with sun-dried tomato essence, all layered into a sourdough tower.' Streaky bacon, mushy pea and ketchup sandwiches it is then.

...when she fills her head with far-fetched schemes courtesy of her fetish for interior-design magazines. The first sign of trouble is when she starts referring to the flat as a 'promising space'. By the time she's muttering about neo-rococo swirls and dropping twigs about the place I'm quietly exiting the 'space' via the back door.

...when she protects me from harm.
'Slow down, you're driving like a madman.'
This as a pair of elderly ladies breeze past on
a tandem and the milk float behind us
toots with impatience.

...when she chooses a video for us to snuggle down and watch together. 'Look, this one's about a couple who overcome a series of heart-breaking near-misses and implausible coincidences before being brought together by their painfully sassy kids.' 'Sounds perfect darling,' I sigh, sliding *Naked Reservoir Ninjas* back on to the top shelf.

...when she falls asleep in my arms.
The agonising cramp that inevitably develops
as the circulation in my arm ceases is a
small price to pay for such moments
of togetherness.

...when she treats me to new clothes.
It makes feel me young again. About nine to
be precise. 'That's right, hold it up, so I can
see if it fits, no don't pull a face, that's it -
now go and ask the lady for some matching
trousers. There's a good boy.'

...when she helps me through the rigours of the working day. It's a great comfort to see the photo of her on my desk smiling encouragingly as I busy myself trying to hit paper ball three pointers into the waste basket and fashion jewellery from paper clips.

...when she concludes a long, meaningful conversation about the sort of things that really matter in our lives, by looking deeply into my eyes and whispering, 'No, I'm sorry - I still don't get "offside".'

...when she gets bizarre pregnancy food cravings. She just can't seem to get enough of stuffed olives. Getting the chocolate inside them isn't easy mind. It's a wonder the sickness only comes in the morning.

...when she helps me remember things. Like our anniversary. I'm unlikely to forget after last year. It's not every morning you roll over to the other side of the bed and find yourself nuzzling a horse's head.

...when she gets into the spirit of things. Whenever we go to a show involving audience participation her hand is always the first to show. Sadly, it's usually clutching my wrist. 'Woo-hoo! Over here! This guy!'

...when she's way smarter than me.
'Darling have you been working out? You're looking good, and this spice rack you made me is magnificent, oh, and have I told you lately how much I love you? Anyhow, can you prepare the spare room for my mother; she'll be here in ten minutes.'

...when she drops little hints.
Like gathering my dirty socks up with a pair of
tongs, dropping them into a clear plastic bag
and muttering something about 'letting the
lab boys have a look at them'.

...when she re-writes the laws of physics. Judging by what goes in and comes out, her handbag would make the Tardis look like a poky bedsit. I peeped in there the other day. There was a faun standing under a lamppost in a winter wonderland. Then Lord Lucan galloped past on Shergar.

...when she shares my interests.
'Now watch this guy. Look at his pace, and great dribbling, use of both feet, great shot and brilliant ball control.' 'Yeah, I see what you mean: nice legs, cute arse and dark, brooding good looks. Is he Italian? I wonder if he can cook?'

...when she teaches me about romance. So now I know that, in that moment of cosy togetherness, on the threshold of sleep, the phrase, 'pull my finger' doesn't, strictly speaking, count as a 'sweet nothing'.